Pretty Precious Poems

Written By
Sophie Parker

MAPLE
PUBLISHERS

Pretty Precious Poems

Author: Sophie Parker

Copyright © Sophie Parker (2024)

The right of Sophie Parker to be identified as author of this work has been asserted by the author in accordance with section 77 and 78 of the Copyright, Designs and Patents Act 1988.

First Published in 2024

ISBN 978-1-83538-316-2 (Paperback)
978-1-83538-317-9 (E-Book)

Cover Design and Book Layout by:
White Magic Studios
www.whitemagicstudios.co.uk

Published by:
Maple Publishers
Fairbourne Drive, Atterbury,
Milton Keynes,
MK10 9RG, UK
www.maplepublishers.com

A CIP catalogue record for this title is available from the British Library.

All rights reserved. No part of this book may be reproduced or translated by any form or by any means, electronic or mechanical, including photocopying, recording or by any information storage and retrieval system without written permission from the author.

The views expressed in this work are solely those of the author and do not necessarily reflect the views of the publisher, and the publisher hereby disclaims any responsibility for them.

CONTENTS

1. Perfect Summers Day 7
2. Love 8
3. Waves 9
4. Home 11
5. Someday 13
6. When? 16
7. A Torment Memory 19
8. Your Heart 21
9. Soulmates 23
10. You 25
11. Suicide 27
12. Family 29
13. Alice in Wonderland 31
14. Alone 33
15. Mothers 34
16. Heaven 36
17. Lonewolf 38
18. Flowers 40
19. The Past 42
20. Castles 43
21. Halloween 44

22. Heartbreak 45
23. Winter 47
24. Being a Teacher 49
25. Christmas 51
26. Warfare 53
27. Being Hunted 55
28. My Love 57
29. Italy 59
30. Camping 60
31. Kibblestone 61
32. Haven 62
33. Funfairs 63
34. The Circus 64
35. Chinese New Year 65
36. Easter 66
37. Bonfire Night 67
38. Fourth July 68
39. Saying Goodbye 69
40. Sherlock Holmes 70
41. Junk Mail 71
42. What's in the box? 73
43. Maybe they had a reason 74
44. In a hospital 75

45. Valentines Day 77
46. England 79
47. Santa 80
48. Nightmares 82
49. Countryside's 84
50. Graduation 85

Sophie Parker

I dedicate this book to Edward Hugh Kirton,
The most loving and kind grandfather anyone could ask for.
And I know one thing for certain,
Seeing you again will be a heavenly cure.
I never want to say goodbye,
Because I know it will my last one.
So, I look up to the sky and breathe with a sigh
Hoping I am making you proud now that you are gone.

Perfect Summers Day

Blooming flowers,
sandcastle towers.
Summertime showers,
long daytime hours.
Ice cream that causes brain freeze,
whilst the sun kisses our skin,
such a tease.

Sand between our toes,
pollen getting up in our nose.
Suncream so thick it sticks to our clothes,
fathers falling into that deep sleeping doze,
as children splash about as the waves arose.

Couples dancing the night away,
children wishing for summer to stay.
Birds dancing along the bay,
Whilst parents wonder where the time went from
August to May.
Blossom trees start to sway,
as all those animals get up to play.
Whilst all these things are great in every way,
It is baked together,
To create a perfect summers day.

Sophie Parker

Love

What is love?
Is it finding the perfect romance,
Or is it finding a partner who can dance?
Is it staying true to yourself,
Or changing ourselves?
Is it finding that spark when you kiss,
Or is it finding that person you just can't resist?

Is love something you can make,
Or is it something you need to take?
Is love to you a need to fake,
Or is love to you have to please for everyone else's sake?
Or is love to you a piece of cake?
Whilst love for others could mean a lot of mistakes.

See love can be tricky,
And loving others can get sticky.
But loving the right one can be a dream,
And loving the wrong one can be a storm upstream.
So, it is important to know what love is about,
Because love is something we all cannot live without.
Love to me is a perfect devout,
And love to me is loving someone through and throughout.

Waves

Waves are beautiful,
Ocean waves crashing against the rocks.
Something so illusional,
Whilst you hang by on the docks.
Sunlight hitting them,
And they gleam and shimmers.
Creatures diving in and out between them,
As the water shines and glimmers.
Swimmers pacing along,
Whilst toddlers splash around.
Waves still going strong,
For surfers to impound,
And ride along like an ocean playground.

Waves can be wonderful,
But dangers, they can hold.
Waves can be harmful,
As their secrets remain untold.
The power they have,
To decide if someone lives or dies.
Is a trick amongst us,
Like a devil in disguise.
Doing it's hardest to win first prize,
Whilst havoc flies.
And the ocean replies,

With its angry eyes,
And its thunderous skies.
This could be the last time we hear your cries.
So, watch out,
As this could be our last goodbye.

But fear not,
The waves are cleaver.
They have their own plot,
And they change whenever.
It all depends on one's feelings.
Anger triggers harsh waves,
Which could imply some deadly dealings.
But a bright soul,
could trigger gentle waves,
Which could make everything go into some control.
And the waves play a great role,
Of being the end goal.
As waves can be a beautifully illusional
And peaceful.

Home

Home is where the heart is,
Or so they say.
But home is more than this,
Home is like a warm summer's day.
A favourite game you like to play,
Beautiful waves crashing into the bay.
Certain smells can also be home.
Smell of a certain someone,
The smell of sweet honeycomb.
Smell of the smoke from a gun,
And the smell of candyfloss,
Reminds me of all the fun.

Home is someone you love,
And being there for a lifetime.
A different kind of true love,
That leaves your heart going overtime.
Makes you stay with them until the end of time.
Some day in the summertime,
With the beautiful butterflies.
Is a home for the heart,
Whereas some say a shade of a sky,
Is a home for someone to restart.
To pick apart,
A broken heart,

And give yourself a kickstart,
Instead of falling apart.
To me home is the sound of the waves,
Crashing along the rocks.
A perfect picture to save,
And a future waiting to unlock.
A dream bigger than the moon,
A wish stronger than the star.
A heartfelt see you soon,
To that special someone.
A home is meant to be happy,
Filled with belly aching laughter.
And even after,
An unhappy chapter,
There can still be hope,
Amongst life's tightrope.
In a home of hope,
In a home of hope.

Someday

Someday,
In the past day.
I was happy,
A cheerful child,
In a wonderful state of mind.
But then,
There came a time when I was sad.
A time I was mad.
A time when I hated the world,
And a moment when I couldn't find,
My own peace and happiness within time.
Pretending to be,
Someone that wasn't me.
Fighting with my emotions daily,
Living a life that was a lie,
To the point I would cry,
To the point I would try,
To die.
Today,
I am stronger.
A fighter.
A survivor.
Of too much power,
Too much confidence,
But it wasn't obvious.

To the girl who loved so much,
Whose soul was broken.
Who got used like a token,
Who was told "I was only jokin".
But little did they know I was choking,
Trying to hold my head high,
Above all the arrogant sighs.
Whilst being stabbed in the back,
By the people you thought loved you.
But only proved your worst fear to be true.
When one scratch turned into two,
Then those two turned into more than a few.
Trauma started forming a que,
To attack me more than most do.
The thought of leaving,
Became a re-accruing proceeding.
Everyday finding it harder to breathe,
Whilst trying to hold onto a reason to not leave.
And I turned into a lost soul,
At a crossroad,
Wondering if it would be better to be gone.
Because this road seems to be too long,
And this thread I'm holding,
Is breaking.

Someday I will be proud.
I will be happier instead of appearing with a frown,
But right now, these voices are too loud,
And I'm sorry you have been let down.
But for now, all I can do is dream,
Of a better time,
Maybe with hot coco and cream.
Graduate.
Make people notice me.
Instead of walking over me.
Someday people will look at me,
And think,
Damn, she might be,
A war worth fighting for.
An open door,
A something more.
Then all the traumas,
Past all the hurtful days,
But until then,
Just gotta keep dreaming,
Of that someday.

Sophie Parker

When?

When?
When will I see you again?
When will I get to hug you?
When will I get to feel again?
Of all the times I spent with you,
All the days filled with joy.
Happiness and laughter,
Making you play with all my favourite toys.
And getting ice cream after,
All those warm cuddles,
Filled with love.
And playing in muddy puddles,
And wearing your shoes like a glove

When will I get that time back?
Before my world turned black.
When will I get to see you smile?
When I know I have done something right.
Instead of walking a mile,
And trying not to cry with all my might.
Wishing you won that fight.
That always makes my chest feel tight.
Cancer never was a friend,
Just an enemy.
Holding your death around the bend,

And you took deaths hand,
That one cold February.
Leaving school to go to your grave.
Even though no one told me why
I was young but not dumb,
But now I gotta be brave.
And ride this tidal wave,
Of being one of griefs slaves.
And remember all the things you gave,
Because your hugs were all I crave,
And you left this beautiful land,
To be somewhere with better sand.

One day when I do see you,
The biggest hug will be given.
The brightest smile is what I will do,
And all the stars will be written.
But until then I will continue to go on,
And do my best to make you proud,
Because until day is dawn,
I will stand out from the crowd.
And sing your name loud,
For all the world to know.
How amazing you are,
And when the time comes,
I will be waiting for you,
Whilst feeling the sun.

That's when I will know,
That's when everything will be done.
That's when I get to see you,
That's when.

A Torment Memory

Every day is just the same.
Same day different pain,
My mood is like the rain.
The question is, when will I be whole again?

Torment memories from the past,
Breaks my heart like its glass.
Didn't take much to shake me,
It's not like a little trauma to break me.

Your name fills the air like daggers,
Whilst I lose balance and stagger.
Your voice beats me to the ground,
Whilst I lay staying still not making a sound.
I pray hoping to be found,
Praying that one day you won't be the reason I'm 6 feet underground.

Thoughts racing through my mind,
Thinking of the days when you used to be kind.
Wishing I can go back in time,
To the day when I wish you would be mine.
Now I look up to the sky,
Thinking if it's better if I just die.
Thinking you would be better off without me,

Sophie Parker

Considering I'm not the girl you wished I be.
I reach for your hand, but you pull away,
Like a child reaching for a parent that doesn't wish to stay.
You tell me it's my fault and that I need to grow up,
I tell you you're wrong and you drag me up.
Your hand clenched around my hair like a last resort,
I cry and scream for you to let me go but I cling onto you like you were life support.

Some people say I should have been stronger,
Then allowed you to hit me harder and harder.
I tried to break free, but you gripped me tighter,
Like a bird trapped in a cage,
But only this time I'm now a fighter.

Your Heart

Your heart.
Something so precious.
Blood flows through,
To refresh us,
And allow us,
To breathe that beautiful air.
Your heart is something that needs a lot of care,
If not, it can give you quite a scare.
Just one little tare,
And you will be needing a hopeful prayer.
Hoping God will spare,
The hurt you might just bare.
You only get one heart.

Your heart is capable of incredible things.
It can make you climb mountain tops,
Sail that boat swaying on the dock.
It can give out love,
To all those who you take care of.
It can treasure those memories,
And hold onto them for centuries.
But if your heart is hurt,
You will need a remedy.
So, you need to be alert,

Sophie Parker

And fight off the poison of your enemy.
As you only got one heart.

The smell of those flowers,
Can make the heart happy.
The height of a tower,
Can make the heart a little snappy.
Different emotions triggers what your heart feels.
So be sure to keep it as healthy as your meals,
As your heart is yours to keep safe.
So, keep it safe,
As you only get one heart.

Soulmates

Soulmates.
What can I say.
It's when two people have more love for each other,
Then they can fit in one single day.
It's holding each other,
Arm in arm,
As they sway.
It's catching each other when one falls.
It's never wanting to miss those persons calls.
It's that person that makes your big problems small,
And it's that person that can break down all your strong walls.

A soulmate makes you feel safe.
A soulmate makes you feel at home.
They can increase your faith,
And say things like "what happens in Rome, stays in Rome".
Those 3 words,
I love you.
Is easy to say with the right person,
And the day they say I do,
Is the day they are soulmates for certain.

Sophie Parker

Your soulmate makes you smile,
And laugh out loud.
Your soulmate might even try to match your style,
And do absolutely everything to try make you proud.
It's the person you never want to let go,
But it's also the person that wants you to grow.
But never let them go,
Because your soulmate is there for life,
Just like those precious vows,
Soulmates keeps us alive.

You

You,
It is always you.
The one to make me smile,
The one to comment on my style.
The day you became mine,
Was a day so fine.
It even made the sunshine.
You changed my life for the better,
Even wants to make me write silly love letters.
You love me when I'm strong,
You love me when I'm weak.
You are the perfect song,
I can listen to all week and on repeat.

Whenever I stand in the crowded room,
I can only think and try to find you.
You are my missing piece.
You are my peace.
My knight in shining armour,
A cheeky charmer.
When you are by my side,
I feel like nothing can get me down.
But when you are not there next to me,
I tend to feel a little lost,

And can't stand tall on this ground,
With my own two feet.

To me you are perfect.
Every day I get with you is a dream come true.
It feels like we were handpicked,
And together there is nothing we can't get through.
It's like we live in a movie screen,
And I can't wait for everything.
I can't wait to spend my life with you,
To say, "I do".
Forever and always.
And for life and all eternity.
I promise to love you,
Through the good and the bad,
For the rest of my days.
I love you for eternity.
It is always going to be you.
Always you,
I love you.

Suicide

Suicide
Never a nice subject.
Always going to reject,
The reality that it reflects,
And the lives that it resets.
The thought process it takes,
For this one decision to make.
The people and everything it forsake,
The feeling you are wished to leave never shakes.
And the never-ending heartache.
No wonder people want a permanent break.

Your brain telling you your worthless,
And that no one will ever love you.
The feeling of being hopeless,
No matter what you try and do.
Never less,
Your trauma lines up one by one in a queue.
The screams of saying I'm helpless,
It's something no one ever wants to go through.
But you're sitting there clueless,
Wondering if everyone has it out to get you.
Thinking of ways to see a better view.
But your mind likes to play tricks,

Saying everything that is said to be true.
Kinda makes you want to start a new.

But I'm sitting here in the dark,
Holding my knees.
Hoping someone can take the chance on me,
Instead of tying a rope,
To then tie to a tall oak tree.
Thinking is this the only way to be free,
Whilst your brain is telling you all the ways you can flee.
You look around hoping someone can notice me,
Instead of walking on by and pretending not to see.
So, I get on up and out this noose around me,
Praying to God that he will be merciful to me.
Smiling and looking up
And knowing I'm about to be free.
I sure hope no one will miss me.

Family

Families.
The one you can rely on.
The ones you can lean on,
And the ones who are with you through the tough times
The sad times.
The ones that love you the most,
And the first ones to toast your victories.

Family teaches you things,
Like love is not a summer fling.
Or how to deal with a little bee sting.
They teach you to be strong,
To not give up.
And although this journey is long,
They make life so much better.
Like putting on your favourite song,
Dancing in the kitchen,
Helping you fix that bike that is always needing a fixing.

Family is an eternal bond.
That always keeps the heart fond.
No matter where you are,
There they are.
Through sickness and in health,
Through light and the dark.

Through the hard times and the wealth.
There are there to hold your hand,
To make it a walk in the park.
To keep your head above water,
And to keep you standing with your head held high.

Family is the everlasting love,
A beautiful gift from the lord above.
Like an olive branch being brought by a dove.
It's something so sacred and full of love.

Pretty Precious Poems

Alice in Wonderland

Alice in wonderland.
What a dangerous game you play.
The Queen being constantly after you,
And here you are wondering what to do.
The white rabbit playing hide and seek,
Whilst you go tripping into a tree trunk.
Yet you can't help but take a peek,
Into the world where you can shrink.

A smiling cat,
The mad hatter and the mouse on his hat.
Tweedledee and Tweedledum,
And the rabbit that looks like he has had too much rum.
Stuck in a world that looks like so much fun,
Until the red Queen releases her hounds that make you run.

The blue caterpillar that looks so high.
Telling you to see the white Queen,
Before hibernating to soon fly.
You hunt the white Queen down,
Who then hands you a sword.
And you can't help but frown,
Because you realise this is a fight where dying is something you can't afford.
So, you pick up your sword with all your might,

To hunt down this red Queen,
Who has her army of cards.
Head-to-head in this fight,
You continue to hold on tight,
As you make the fatal blow,
That win the feud.
And everyone cheers like it has been queued.
Next thing you know you are back by that tree trunk.
Wondering if it was real or a bad dream where you got stuck.

So, you wonder back.
Looking back,
Hoping that white rabbit shows its face.
But now you have a whole family to on your case.
Time to make a choice,
Time to use your voice.
But as you go to speak,
The other world goes to make a creak.
And whispers Alice is needed in wonderland.
What a dangerous game you have played
Alice from wonderland.

Alone

Alone
All alone.
Sitting here with my thoughts,
Chilling with my dark parts.
Trying to find happiness is harder than popping a balloon with a dart.
One moment your happy,
Next, I'm feeling crappy.
And then I'm feeling sad,
And next I'm feeling bad.
Wishing to receive all the things I never had.
My demons whispering to me in my head,
Making me never mind want to leave my bed.
Wishing I was dead.
Then reliving those midnight memories inside my head.

No one around me,
Just how I like it.
But there's one part of me that wishes I could never feel it.
It is always a troubling thought.
That dances around my heart.
This feeling of being alone,
Is like walking in an endless dead zone.
If only I could pick up the phone,
To end being alone.

Sophie Parker

Mothers

Mothers.
Such a blessing to have.
Mothers,
A love that will always grow beyond the grave.
She will love you no matter what.
She will give you everything she has got.
Cuddles in your cot and cuddles you without a second thought.

She is always the first to say I love you.
A home cooked meal is what she will always do.
Pinning up the pictures you drew,
And making you smile whenever those tears decided to come and go.
Always telling us to tie your shoes,
And reminding us to say our P and Q's.
Helping us with that spelling bee,
Teaching us to be free,
And telling us not climb up that tree.
Making us see the world how she sees,
How beautiful a planted garden could be.

She scarifies evening for us.
Even if it hurts her.
She places all her trust upon us.
Whilst wrapping us in cotton wool,
Protecting us.
And she will be by your side when you say I do.
And hold your hand when times get tough.
Helps you through all that baby stuff.

She is a miracle on earth.
A beautiful gift from above.
A treasure given since birth.
And she is always there,
With all her care
And with her everlasting love.

Sophie Parker

Heaven

Heaven,
It's like a breath of fresh air,
A moment of calm and fun ride at the funfair.
It's like a perfect summers day,
It makes you feel warm and fuzzy,
In a wonderful way.

There are birds singing in the trees,
And leaves that dance in the wind like they are free.
There are white sand beaches,
With oceans that glisten so bright the whole world can see.
There really is nowhere else you would rather be.

He is there at the gates with open arms.
It's like a feeling of relief in your very own way palms.
He is the one true father to us all,
Because no matter what we do,
He is always there to catch us when we fall.
He teaches us even when we are in the middle of a storm,
And we need to stand tall.
He is always there when we just need to make that one special call.

So heaven is more than a place called home.
It's a beautiful land to face,
And it's where all our family have been watching us with grace.
It's a blessing to us wrapped up in love,
From the ultimate parents from way up above.

Sophie Parker

Lonewolf

Lonewolf,
That's what they call me.
I am always alone,
Rather nobody bothers me.
I'd prefer to be alone,
Because I have never been good in crowds.
They are just far too loud.
People today are just too proud,
They got their heads stuck in a cloud.
To them I'm a reject,
So, I like to sit back and reflect.
Ever since the day I decided to reset,
My life in order to protect,
My heart
It feels perfect.
When I walk on in,
They don't know who I am.
For all this time,
I have racked up so many sins.
But seriously who cares,
They sure don't care.
I almost break out a grin,
Because to everyone I am a disease.
Constantly unable to please,
These people it's like they want to keep me on a leash.

But I never got in.
Ever since I was a child.
But being an outcast always made me smile.
Because the thought of being invisible to them,
It a dream,
No, it's a perfect plan.
You see it wasn't just the root that failed me,
It was the stem.
They failed me as a person.
And they never learn,
So now I'm sitting in the shadows cursing,
Almost everyone around me.
Thinking to myself,
I might be lonely,
But at least I'm free,
To be me.

Sophie Parker

Flowers

Flowers
They pop up in the spring,
Oh, such joy that they bring.
It's a wonderful thing,
That even make the birds sing.
It fills our hearts with joy,
To know something so beautiful that we can enjoy.
That makes out gardens colourful,
With roses, pansies, dandelions, and a daisy.
So, to receive them can be cheerful,
And it sure does make the bees crazy.
As the wind dances around them,
Whilst the rain helps to grow and sing.
And the sun shining so bright upon them,
Which makes it perfect to pick.
Especially to propose with a ring.

But once plucked,
They only got a week.
Before they start to get weak
And crumble beneath our feet.
But if we take care of them,
They can last a few more weeks,
Before the circle of life comes to an end.
They are so delicate,

It's true happiness.
It's almost like a testament,
A warm feeling inside us.
So, remember when the flowers bloom,
To enjoy them,
When the dark days gloom.
Because it's time to consume,
All that joy.
Because it can fill a room,
Like a favourite perfume,
The flowers that bloom.

Sophie Parker

The Past

The past.
Something we can't relive.
But it's something we can give.
Away to someone else,
So, all those heavy burdens we may carry on our shoulders.
Can be lifted, so we can try start over.

But the past can hold some power.
All that heritage in our history,
We can soon unravel this mystery.
Or it could loom over us,
Like a tall tower of shame.
It can even bring us so much pain,
And feel like you have chains.
That can break us.
Yet, if we send up a prayer,
Our chains can be broken.
He is like our own demon slayer,
And nothing can be left unspoken.

But the past is the past,
It just happens so fast.
And sometimes you need to leave the past,
To enjoy the present and relax at last,
And leave everything in the past.

Castles

Castles.
They hold so much history,
So much mystery,
Of those who came before us.
And ruled our land,
So precious.
Stone walls still standing strong,
Almost like nothing went wrong,
But some castles weren't as strong.
It's like a war destroyed it,
Like a heartbreak song.
It's where fantasy stays all day long,
And mysteries wait to be found,
Along this old abandoned,
Castle ground.

Sophie Parker

Halloween

Welcome all,
To Halloween.
A special holiday in the fall,
That will make you scream.
The wind piercing through your hair,
And fingers waiting to grab you under the stairs.
The ghouls hiding under your bed,
Whilst sirens play with the thoughts in your head.
All these things starts making you wish you were dead.

Pumpkins carvings on your floor,
Trick or treaters at your door.
Spirits start playing with fire,
As the pumpkin king, summons the devil.
Everyone will be calling you a liar,
When you start seeing the devil and his demons causing peril.
Because nothing else will make you scream
On this night of Halloween.

Heartbreak

Heartbreak.
Nothing breaks like a heart,
And I believe them.
You tore my whole world apart.
I thought you were such a gem,
And here we are now,
Parted ways.
And already found someone else to make me say wow.
As I threw that ring far into the ocean bay.
What a waste now.

I know I am never going to fall in love with you again.
We both broke promises
And now I must regain.
The self-respect I lost to protect.
And use this time of this heartbreak to reflect.
And reject.
Anyone who might remotely come close to me.
Because saying goodbye now seemed to be,
The only easy thing from this heartbreak for me.

Sophie Parker

It's always the after,
From an unhappy chapter.
That leaves you broken,
Leaves you helpless.
And hopeless.
Wondering if the relationship was doomed from the start.
But since we grew apart,
There really has been nothing much that has mended this broken heart.

Winter

Winter,
It's a beautiful season.
Snow falling on the ground.
Making snow angels for no reason,
But to laugh in the cold.
Throwing snowballs until someone folds.
And no eating yellow snow,
At least that's what I'm told.
Yet eating snow cones,
Now I'm sold.

Wrapping up warm in blankets by the fire.
Time to grab those skis from the shop to hire.
Hot chocolate with marshmallows and cream,
Whilst thinking of a winter wonderland.
Oh, what a dream.
Cuddling close to loved ones.
Whilst mothers and fathers make your favourite roast.
Now that's my kind of homerun.

People bringing out their winter gear.
Whilst the frozen lake might fill someone with fear.
Ice skating may not be for everyone,
But playing board games,
Now that sounds like fun.
This season among us is a whole new level,
As the winter season,
Is just so special.

Being a Teacher

Being a teacher is a special job for someone to do.
Children learn to trust you,
And you're paid to teach them everything you knew.
Whilst putting on that smiley show.
For anyone that comes close to,
Learn from you.

Some days though are hard.
Kids sometimes disregard all your rules.
And parents are here thinking you are the fool.
For not making their children learn,
Man, that's cruel.
Even though they have too much energy to burn,
And choose not to listen to you.
The devils card always seems to be played on your turn.
I mean seriously, what are you meant to do.
You can hit them or touch them,
You will get sued.
Gotta keep trying to feed them kindness.
And hope it gets through.

However, there are some dangers.
Like accidentally letting in a stranger,
Who might make threats.
Who only wishes to pay off his or her debts.

But some teachers must face that gun.
That put a weight on your heart which can feel like a ton.
The children are safely locked away in a different room,
As you hope to God,
This pressing matter will end soon.
But there's not a lot you can do.
Except feed kids candy to keep them quiet.
As you pray and do everything, they want you to.

See being a teacher is more than you think.
It's not a walk in a park.
As it will make you rethink,
The challenges you might embark.
Of being a teacher.
So, it's time to think,
If being a teacher is for you,
Because sometimes being a teacher,
Is doing more than what is asked of you.

Christmas

Christmas.
It fills the air with magic,
As red, green, and gold lights up the room.
Listening to last Christmas,
What a classic.
So much chocolate to consume,
And mistletoe coming into bloom.
Love is lingering with that in the room.

People picking their tallest tree to break free,
And decorate with baubles and lights.
It makes the room so bright,
And fills our hearts with delight.
Presents gathering under the tree,
As children try sneak a peek.
Big presents are what they try to seek.
Children leaving carrots, whiskey, and mince pies,
For Santa to come and try.
Children will try to stay up all night,
To try catch him in plain sight.
But they always fall asleep,
No matter how hard they try,
It's a memory they will keep.

Parents stand by with huge bin bags,
To catch the wrapping paper.
Children with happy faces as they see that one present,
That says it's from Santa and his favourite helper.
Christmas dinner brings all the family together,
For this special day where they give thanks and gather.
To Jesus Christ that was born that day,
Because Christmas wouldn't be here without him,
Which is special in every single way.
Time to celebrate this magical Christmas Day.

Warfare

Warfare
Always gives people a scare,
Families it will always tare.
As they always need soldiers to spare,
But what do they care?
Mothers and fathers tell them to take care,
Wondering if life would ever be fair.
Countries going into war,
And everyone is closing their door.
Hoping there won't be any more,
But building keep crashing and crumbling down to the floor.
And bloodshed is all around,
As soldiers fall everywhere on the ground.

Now soldiers continue firing their guns at the enemy,
Whilst the enemy keep their targets on the innocent.
Bodies that can no longer be identified
And people losing their ligaments.
Just makes them wonder what they could have done different.
Whilst those who are lost,
Suffer with the ignorance,
Of those of the world who would rather help themselves than help the others.
Makes you scream so loud,
But nothing is heard just silence.

Warfare causes so many deaths.
That makes us wonder if it is worth all this trouble.
Fire and rescue are constantly pulling bodies out of rubble.
And making those calls to family,
Causes a pounding in their chests.
And a raging inside their heads.
Because war does nothing but cause conflict
And it makes you heart flip.
Because nothing can be accomplished
From a warfare that cannot be won from a permanent bed.

Being Hunted

Running through the tall oak trees.
Trying not to trip.
Scrapes all over your knees
As death tries to get ahold of your grip.
All you want is to be safe and sound,
But you have to keep racing on this uneven ground.
That makes your heart pound,
And your head spin round and round.

The fear of being caught
Is a whole lot.
The sound of a gunshot,
Causes your stomach to knot.
This is something you know you can't outrun,
As the thought of the person catching you with the finger on their gun.
Is nothing but fun.
But you make the wrong turn
As they catch up to you.
Shouting it's your time to burn.
You scramble to the best you can to try get away,
But they are stronger than you are.
And it's the middle of the day.

Sophie Parker

You are still so very far away
For anyone to hear your screams
But they raise the gun to your head
And you think does it hurt being dead?
And before they pull the trigger,
They ask if there is anything left to be said.
But you wake up suddenly as you scream,
Sweating and panting
Because the thought of being hunted is nothing but a bad dream.

My Love

My Love
What can I say,
The day I got with you was the very best day.
You will always be the one,
My number one.
Your love is all I need,
And now I see,
Anywhere with you is a home to me.

My heart beats for you.
I will love you for this life and a thousand more.
I am yours and you are mine hand in hand,
We will make the world around us shine.
Butterflies every time I kiss you,
My arms locked around you.
You make me better than I ever was before.
And I thank God every day that get to be yours.

You might have said it first,
Those three little words.
But I hope I am your last.
We all have a Rocky past,
But you won't scare me away.
So let that storm come anyway,

Because I ain't going nowhere.
And there is nothing out love cannot bare.

You mean the world to me,
You are my destiny.
You are my missing piece,
And my forever peace.
It's a million things about you,
That makes me love you.
Because I have never known a love like this,
That makes me dream of our very first kiss.
That makes me dream of the day I say I do.
You're my everything and I hope I am yours too.
You are my love, and there's nothing I'd rather do,
Then spend eternity next to you.

Italy

Italy,
What a wonderful place.
With the sun kissing your face,
And tourists heading to the beach like it's a race.
People buying wine by the case,
And they drink at such a fast pace,
No wonder most are smashed and off their face.

Pizzas cooking in the fire,
And olives and bread are the fabulous starter.
That pasta mountain on the plate,
Always gets higher and higher,
Whilst the birds sing in the trees like a choir.
The mountain views are a beauty to see,
Just like being in little Italy.

Sophie Parker

Camping

People camping in their vans,
Whilst the hardcore campers pitch their tents.
A weekend of eating out of cans,
And maybe some sweets that your mother sent.
Creating a fire from logs in the wood,
As the wind picks up, you put up your hood.
As you sit around the fire to get as warm as you could,
You bring out the s'mores that are deliciously good.
And by the end of the night when your tucked up in your tent,
Kids smiling thinking it's the best time they have ever spent,
And you will think that maybe this was the best idea yet.

Kibblestone

Workers in purple jumpers,
To entertain those very keen campers.
Who loves an outdoors challenge,
Whilst the children find conkers to scavenge.
A high ropes course that gives people a fright,
Whilst the axe throwing uses all your might.
Archery needs your best sight,
But target shooting is one you need to aim just right.
Rafting for all the water lovers,
And Nightline that needs your eyes to be covered.
All these activities and more at your door,
Will make you wanting to come back for more.
Big campfires are built for warm pleasure,
And children seek the gift shop for some local treasure.
The peace and quiet here is anything but seldom,
As the Kibblestone staff gives you a very warm welcome.

Sophie Parker

Haven

Haven summers are just the best,
It puts your skills to the test.
Lots of activities for everyone to choose,
And families go up against each other to see who will lose.
The splashaway bay includes those thrilling water slides,
Whilst the sports drome has roller skates for people to try.
The Segways are fun to ride and glide,
And the bug hunt offers a chance to find the bugs that hide.
Entertainment is offered to all ages,
As the singers and dancers take over the stages.
Lots of food takeouts to try,
But doughnuts from the sweet treats is what I will buy.
Bunnies and bees take over the land,
As families spend their days on the sand.
Everyone who works for Haven can humbly agree,
A breath of fresh air describes Haven down to a tee.

Funfairs

Going to the fair can be so much fun,
There are so many rollercoasters to choose from.
Some people like hitting metal horses with guns,
To try win the largest teddy that weighs a ton.
The Ferris wheel could be seen as a couple's ride,
Whereas the haunted house is the perfect place to hide.

People enjoy going round and round the carousel,
Kids who are too small go on their tiptoes so workers can never tell.
Candyfloss, popcorn, and Hot Dogs too,
Are all funfair treats you can choose.

The river rapids will get you wet,
Whilst the smiler and Rita is as thrilling as it gets.
As days go on and rides get ridden again and again,
It's true to say a funfair is a favourite for all to attend.

Sophie Parker

The Circus

The circus can be a favourite time,
As ques of people wait patiently in a line.
People come from all over the world,
To see the show that is about to be untold.

Ringmasters open up the event,
In a huge red and white tent.
Aerobatics swinging from ropes high up,
As a contortionist can fit into spaces as small as a tiny cup.
Colours and lights fill the arena,
As mime artists make you become a believer.
Clowns enter out of the crowd,
As screams and laughter become their favourite sound.

Elephants trying to balance on a ball,
As people on stilts are seen as very tall.
Some have tigers and lions locked in a cage,
That seem to always take the stage.
And when all the fun and laughter is done,
The circus remains the most fun.

Chinese New Year

Dragons enter the crowded streets,
As the people viewing the show are in for a treat.
Chicken chow mein for the couple over there,
And sticky ribs for the bloke with eye watering stare.
Some smile, some frown and some can't bare,
As the fortune cookies are not always fair.
Kids munching on many prawn crackers,
As the crispy duck remains the real lip smacker.
Whilst finding your year is fun to be told,
Chinese New Year is exciting to celebrate all over the world.

Sophie Parker

Easter

As Palm Friday passes and Easter Sunday arrives,
We remember Jesus Christ,
Who sacrificed and died.
He then arose on Day three,
Just seems miraculous to me.

Chocolate eggs are given out,
As the easter bunny hops about.
Easter egg hunts are for all ages,
As one egg hides in the rabbit cages.

A nice lamb dinner sounds lush to me,
As we give thanks and remember thee.
No matter what the weather,
It always brings family together.
As the easter traditions remains standing tall,
It's safe to say,
Easter is important to all.

Bonfire Night

People gather wood from all around,
To build the biggest bonfire on the ground.
As the creative skills are put to the test,
To see who will win the Guy Fawkes contest.
Workers put the dolls on the fire,
For everyone to see and admire.
We remember the guy who is famous in British history,
Why he would do it is still a mystery.

Fireworks explode with all colours in the sky,
As the pulled pork baps catches my eye.
Sparklers glisten in the night,
To make bonfire night a pretty sight.
As families cozy up by the fire,
And hot chocolates and as many marshmallows as they desire,
We think about the next years bonfire.

Sophie Parker

Fourth July

Fourth July is a special day,
At least that is what the Americans say.
Independence is a cause for celebration,
As red, white and blue are the new colours in creation.
American flags waving in the air,
As fireworks are being handled with care.
Families being brought together,
No matter what the weather.
Food and drink turn into a beautiful banquet.
Chocolate cake seems to the children's favourite fit.
As the night rolls in and the fireworks alight,
It causes the sky to be a pretty sight,
As we remember those who fought with all their might.

Saying Goodbye

Saying goodbye is a hard thing to do,
It is something people wish you never had to do.
The pain you go through,
The heartache that pulls you down.
The depression which causes you to frown,
And never wanting to leave that cozy dressing gown.
All because those tears could then flood the whole town,
But saying goodbye doesn't mean forever.
If you are meant to be together.

You can,
You will,
See them again.
Your loving gran,
And that one best friend,
Just wish life never had an end.
But hope keeps us living,
And the keepsakes are a comforting love,
And they keep on giving.
Yet those tears in your eyes,
Always fall at the word goodbye.
As they look one last time at the sky,
And you watch their angel wings fly.
Hoping all your family are all together up there,
But saying goodbye doesn't mean forever, right?

Sophie Parker

Sherlock Holmes

Down on Baker Street,
Theres a man who loves impossible mysteries,
 Who you will meet.
His name is Sherlock Holmes,
So, take a seat,
As there is nothing he cannot solve.

From a small, tiny clue,
He will know what to do.
Weather its Moriarty playing a game,
Or Adler trying to spy on the government.
Sherlock's mind palace remains the same,
Which helps reach his achievements,
And find out who is to blame.

But we cannot forget his trusty companion,
Watson the right - hand man champion.
Who never leaves his side,
Through every bumpy ride.
Sherlock is quite the famous figure,
Who always must consider,
What makes the enemy pull their trigger.
With each clue getting bigger and bigger,
Sherlock and Watson must solve the crime,
But can they solve it in time?

Junk Mail

Junk Mail,
I wonder what people are trying to sell.
Let's open one and see,
Win an iPad, sounds dodgy to me.
Next,
Join Cynthia in the eighteen plus group that has just sent,
Not my kind of entertainment.
I will pass.

Do you need a body part enlargement?
Why do people keep trying to make me better with these enhancements?
Ooo, this looks good.
I can give you all these goodies for free,
All I need is your card details.
I wonder how many times that has failed.

Another one here we go,
Buy one phone get your next five free,
Another scam I see.
Let's keep scrolling.
Don't chop down the trees,
Was not my intention honestly.
Last one.

Sophie Parker

Need a lawyer, I am the guy for you,
Right, but what did I do?

See junk mail always tries to trick us,
But we got to be smarter,
Otherwise, we can be crying on the bus,
Looking at the money we just lost.
Which made us rethink,
Maybe I shouldn't have clicked that one link.

Pretty Precious Poems

What's in the box?

What's in the box?
Is it a teddy bear?
Or is it something I can tear?
Could it be those trousers that flare?
Or is it a button that became a spare?
Is it something that needs to be handled with care?
Or is it a mask I can use to try give my siblings a scare?
What about something that will give me long hair?
This is such a mystery.

Could it be something from the past?
Or a cake that won last?
What about a nerf gun I can blast?
This is bugging me more than when I had a cast.
Look, I really need to know,
As the desire to know is starting to grow.
So, tell me Mr. Box,
What is inside your box?

Sophie Parker

Maybe they had a reason

Maybe they had a reason,
To not stay.
Winter has always been the coldest season.
Didn't think it was your heart that was going to go astray.
Maybe they a reason to leave,
And not show up for my birthday.
I know that feeling of hard to breathe,
Wishing they would just return someday.
Maybe they had a reason to abandon me,
And leave me feeling hopeless and alone.
It is definitely the worst they could do,
Especially not seeing how much I have grown.

Maybe they had a reason,
To throw away their one shot,
At knowing you and the wonderful life can be.
Maybe a few years is all you both could handle,
Because you are now sat crying under a tree,
Wondering did they leave because of me?
But maybe they had a reason to leave,
Maybe it's a reason we just simply cannot understand,
And maybe this just wasn't part of their plan.
Maybe they made a mistake,
At being known as nothing to you but a fake.
But what if maybe, just this once,
Just maybe they had one good reason.

In a hospital

It is always scary,
Being in hospital.
Everyone is aways weary,
If they are going to go critical.
It is not an easy feeling,
Knowing you are unwell.
You just got to keep believing,
That you will rise from where you fell from.

Sometimes the heart cannot take it,
The pain it goes through.
And sometimes that bitter pill you had to swallow,
As everything becomes hollow,
Hearing that cancer is on your path to follow.
Although sometimes surgery will be the deed,
And surgeons will fight so hard.
But you took the chance to be freed,
As death played his final card.

However, not all is bad,
Newborns are born here too.
It is a blessing,
To have such a miracle happen right in front of you,

Sophie Parker

The miracle of childbirth.
So, yes hospitals can be scary and sad,
But they can be happily and joyful upon this earth.
Because in a hospital anything can happen.
It is one experience, yet to be had.

Valentines Day

Valentines Day,
A day filled with love,
And some might say,
It's a gift from above.
Falling in love with their eyes,
And stealing kisses behind closed doors.
It is like winning a prize,
And having your name on Hollywood floor.
It fills up your heart,
And makes you want to buy a rose.

A ring in a cake is a wonderful start,
For someone to propose.
Making the bed,
Making shapes with petals,
And cooking candlelit dinners for two.
Let's just say that ring better be real metal,
As we all know what is awaiting next for you.

Valentines Day is making your other half feel appreciated and special,
And holding onto them tight.
Because after the day is done,

Sophie Parker

You will never want to leave their sight.
As the love is stronger than might,
And this love is worth the fight,
So, Valentines Day needs to be done right.

England

Red and white flags for all to see.
As mum and dad sits down with their cups of tea.
Fish and chips make the perfect supper,
Maybe just one more cuppa?
Jam and cream with some cherry scones,
Castle ruins for children to roam.
Playing make believe like they were knights in Rome,
And the rainy weather never keeps some from leaving their home.

Motorways are the absolute worst,
The long ques just make you want to curse.
Big Ben, The London Eye and Madam Tussauds,
Some of the most favourite tourist place to see.
Whereas some who like a thrill will seek Alton Towers or the London Dungeon,
Well, that is where I will be.
With the pub being everyone's favourite place,
England is for sure my kind of taste.

Sophie Parker

Santa

Santa Clause,
Have I been naughty or nice?
I know you have a list,
And that you are checking it twice.
I know you are busy preparing for the big day,
And making sure all the gifts can fit in your sleigh.
Some eleves making sure that the star shines bright,
Which leads to the north pole.
Hoping that Rudolph leads the reindeer with all his might,
To bring joy to all souls.

I know to leave you a mince pie,
And a carrot for the reindeer.
I am going to make sure my stocking is pinned up high,
And wondering where abouts you are in the sky.
Staying up late hoping I see you and the reindeer fly,
But when clocks strike midnight,
I will make sure I am tucked in bed out of sight.
Down the chimney,
Into our homes to drop off the gifts.
Hopefully I get everything on my list.

As the day sets to arise,
We no longer see the star in the sky,
But there is Christmas spirit throughout the world on this day.
As we continue to remember you and the baby boy asleep on the hay,
Christmas is special,
What can I say.

Sophie Parker

Nightmares

Nightmares,
They always make me scared.
The positions they put me in,
Creating sin,
But where do I begin?

I had one where I was drowning,
Another has my family frowning.
It is like the devil wears the crown,
And runs this whole town.
As I keep running inside my mind,
Constantly trying to find,
Someone who will be kind.
Instead of this nightmare stuck on rewind.

Another nightmare happened,
It is where I was kidnapped.
I was stuck underground,
Trapped.
Unable to move,
Unable to breathe.
It is then I start to grieve,
Because it feels so real,

I might actually die.
The pain hurts so much to not feel,
The anxiety it causes,
Which causes me to cry.

So, sometimes I can't sleep,
Because I don't want that feeling,
Of never getting out.
Never getting rid,
Of this nightmare,
That still stands tall and walks about.

Sophie Parker

Countryside's

Farmland as far as the eye can see,
Not many neighbourhoods near me.
Sheep in the field next to you,
Wildflowers adding colour in the sun where they grew.
Birds singing their favourite song,
As the vegetable patch keeps coming along.
Beans, tomatoes, courgettes and potatoes too,
All homegrown and ready to eat.
As the quiet surrounding you,
Is something you just can't beat.
As people race by to admire to beauty it brings,
There is nothing quite like the countryside,
To relax from all the big and little things.

Graduation

Graduation,
A celebration so true,
Seeing your parents being so proud of you.
Having your classmates by your side,
As you endure your last time as a cohort together.
The past three or four years have been a crazy ride,
But they hold memories that will last a forever.

The feeling of walking across that red carpet,
As they call your name.
As your shake the counsellor's hand,
And you embrace those few moments of fame.
Throwing your caps in air,
Getting photos with those who care.

As you feel a big relief to finally be done,
You can now relax,
Continue forward and have fun.
As you think to yourself,
Of how much you have won,
Realising that your graduation is done.
Now the very best is yet to come.

www.ingramcontent.com/pod-product-compliance
Lightning Source LLC
Chambersburg PA
CBHW072105110526
44590CB00018B/3321